How To Draw Realistic Skulls Volume 8

Simple Guide to Drawing Skulls

How to Draw Skulls

By : Gala Publication

Published By :

Gala Publication

© Copyright 2015 – Gala Publication

ISBN-13: **978-1522786061**
ISBN-10: **1522786066**

Table of Contents

4

CHRISTMAS SKULL

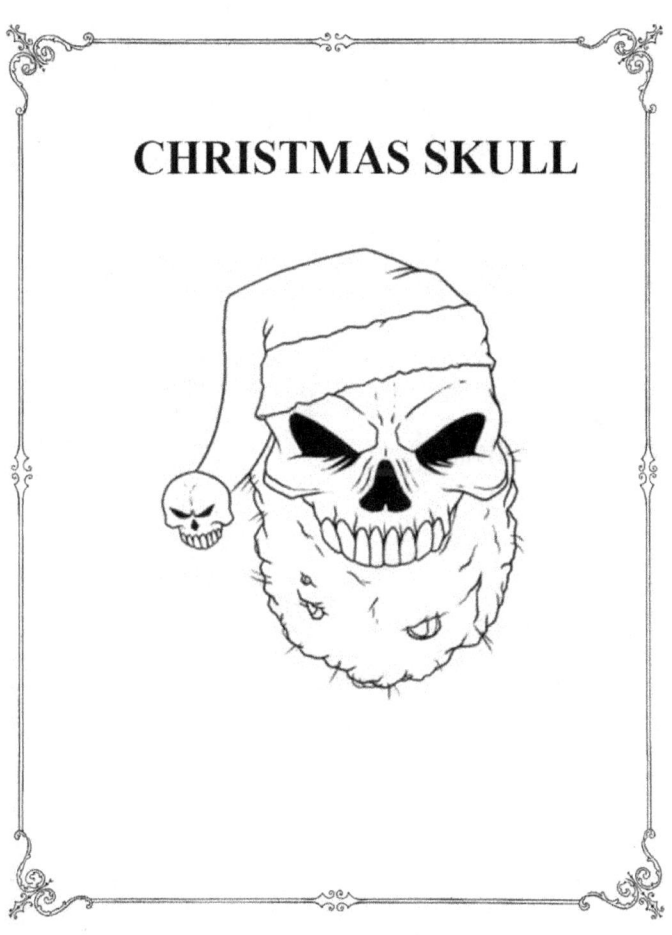

STEP 1

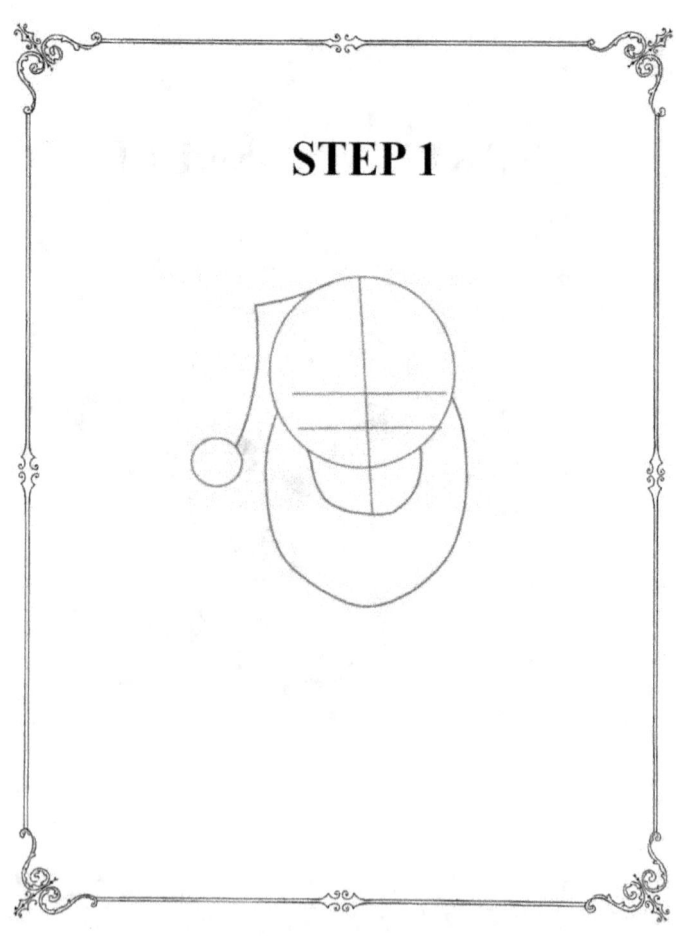

STEP 2

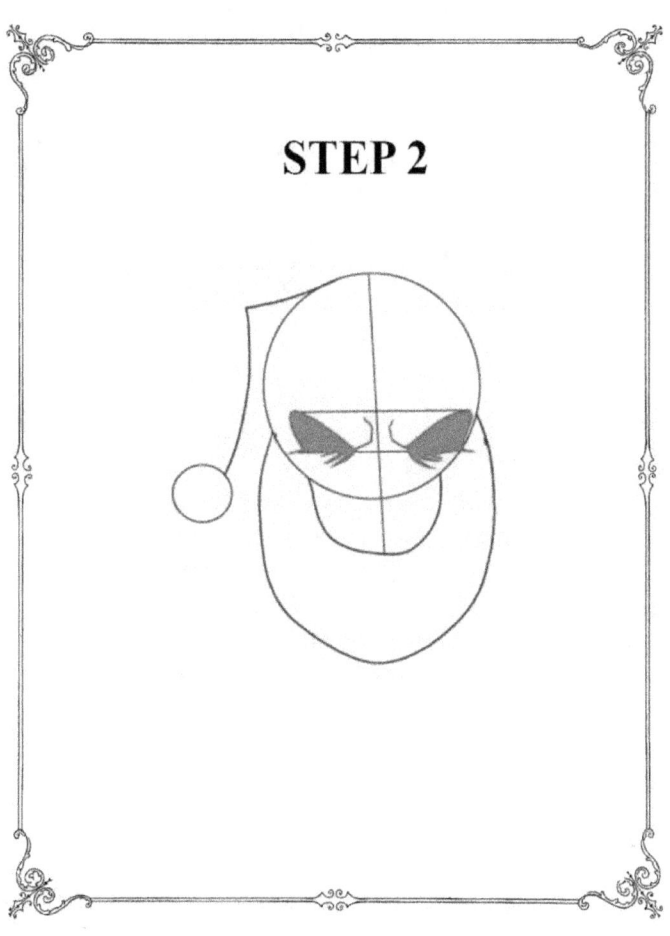

STEP 3

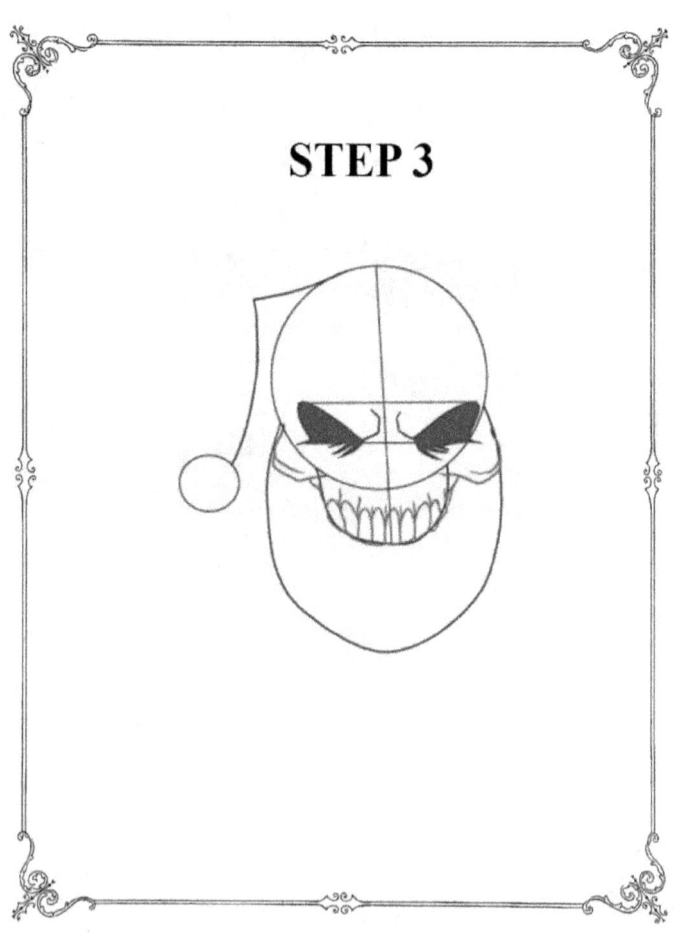

STEP 4

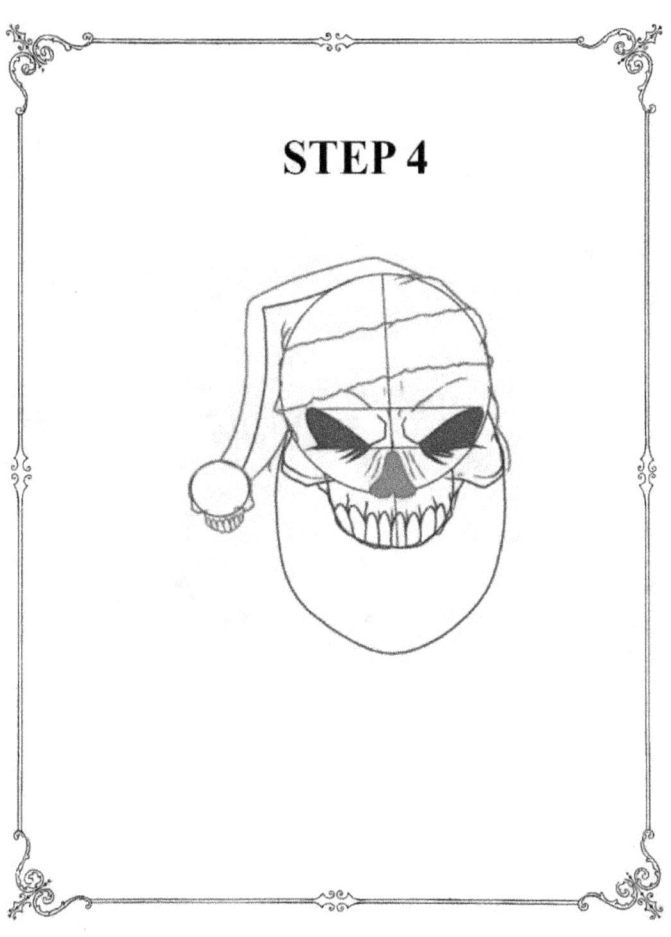

STEP 5

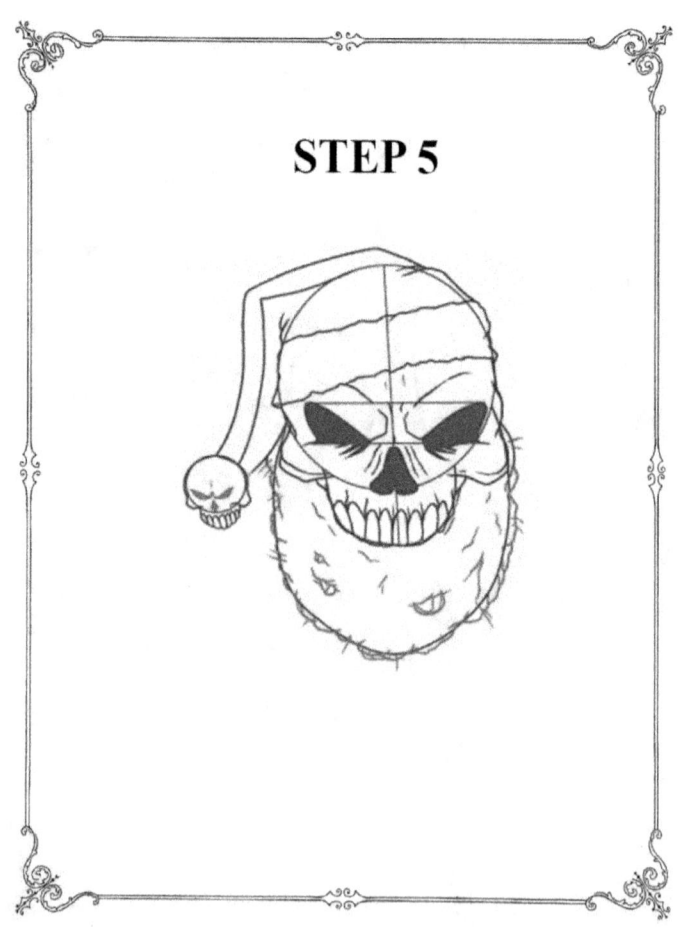

STEP 6

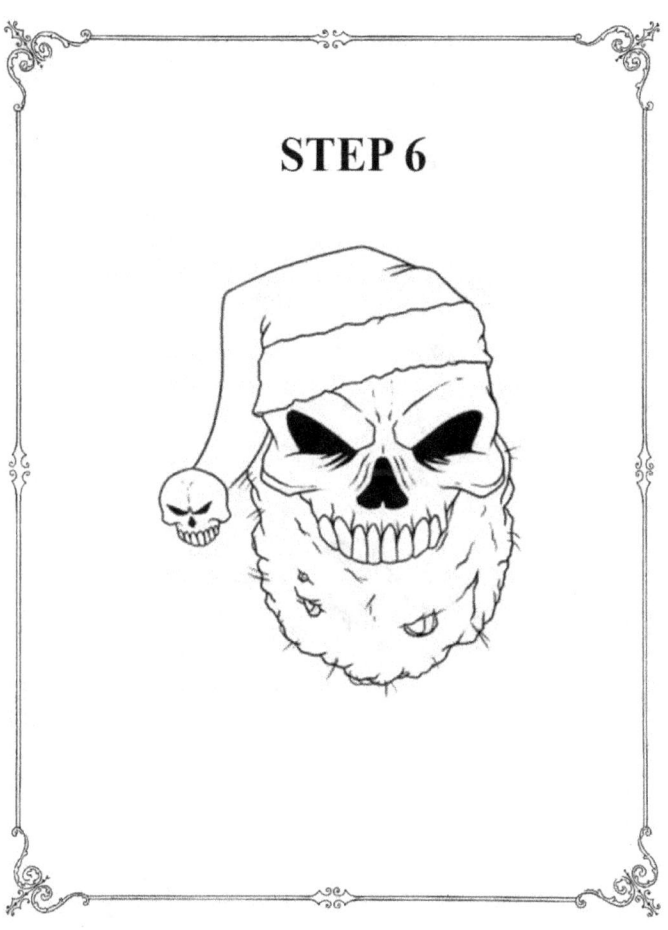

CLASSIC SKULL

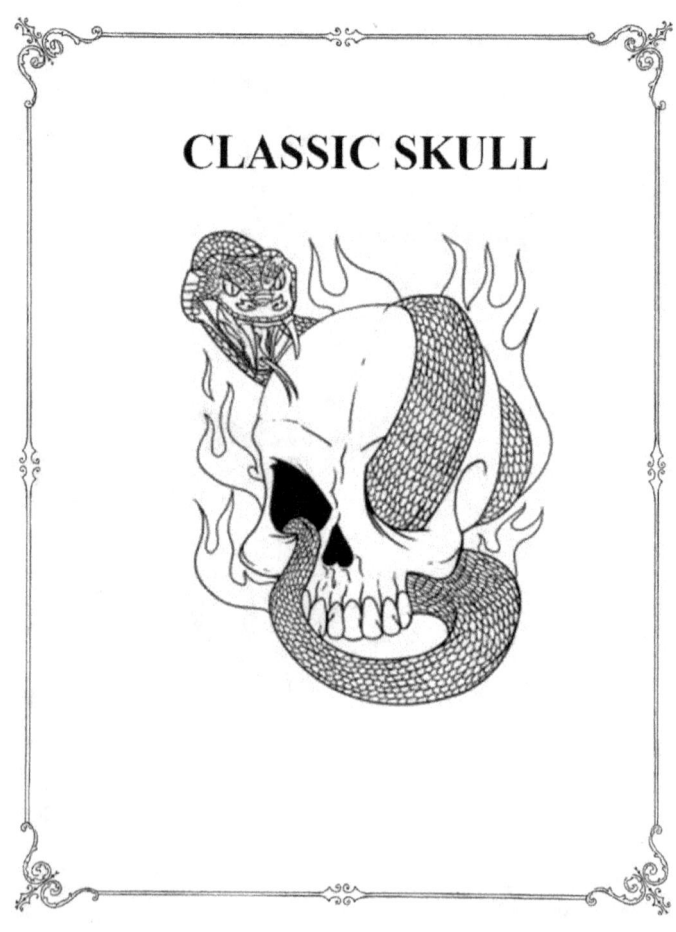

STEP 1

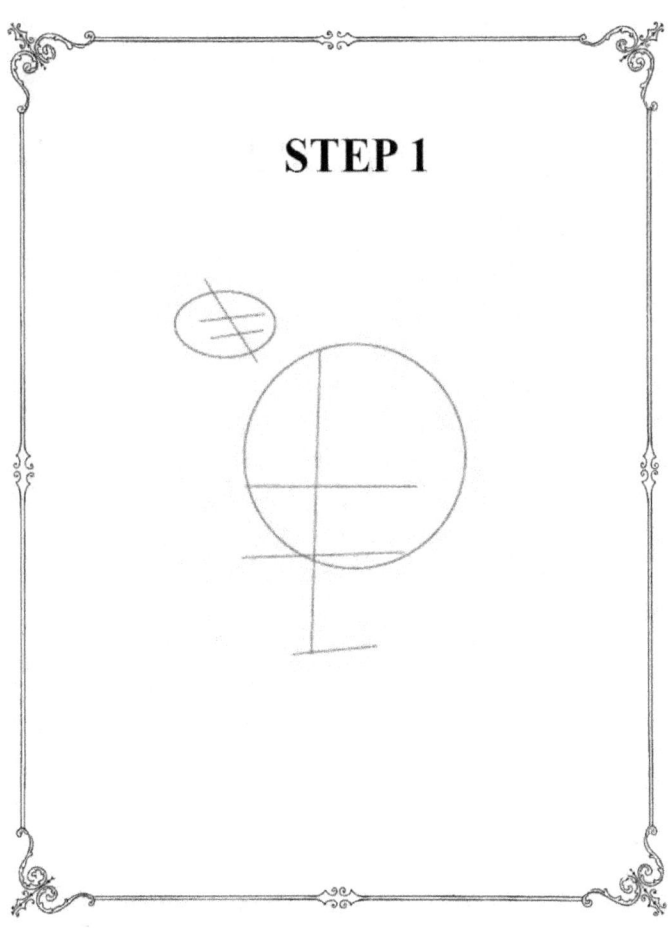

STEP 2

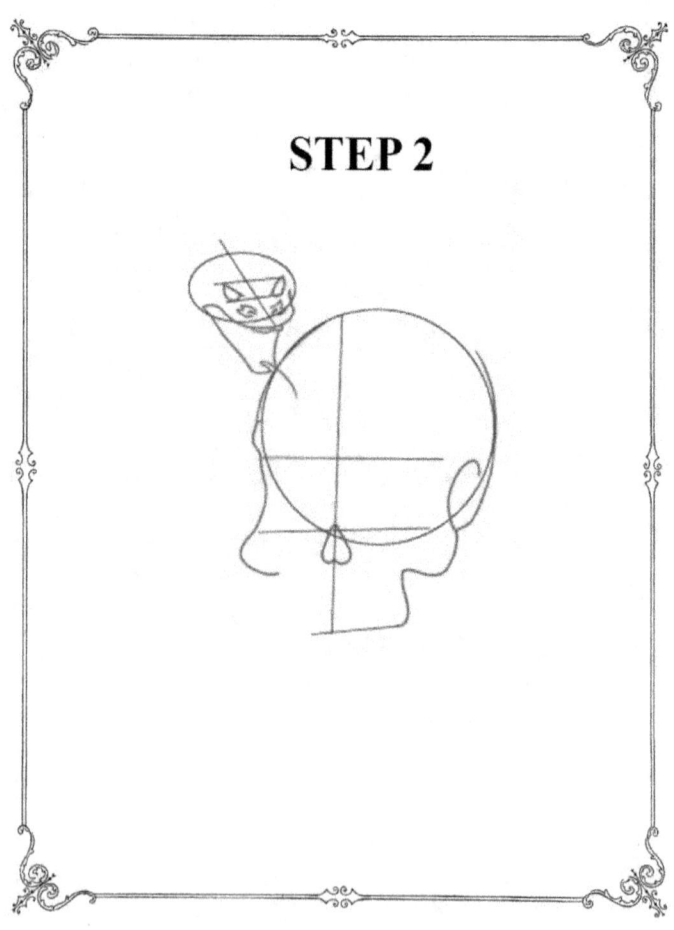

STEP 3

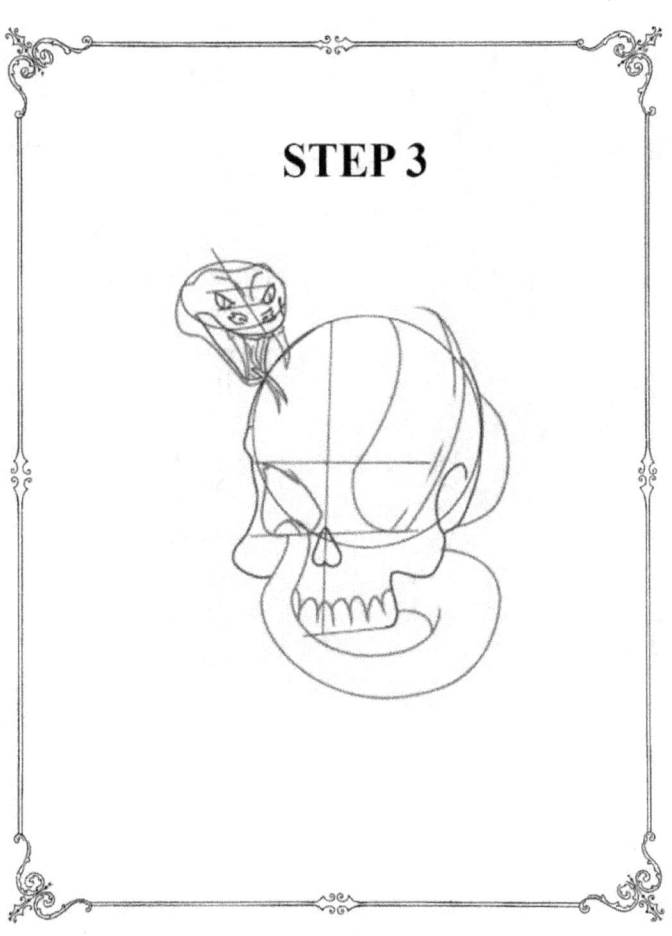

STEP 4

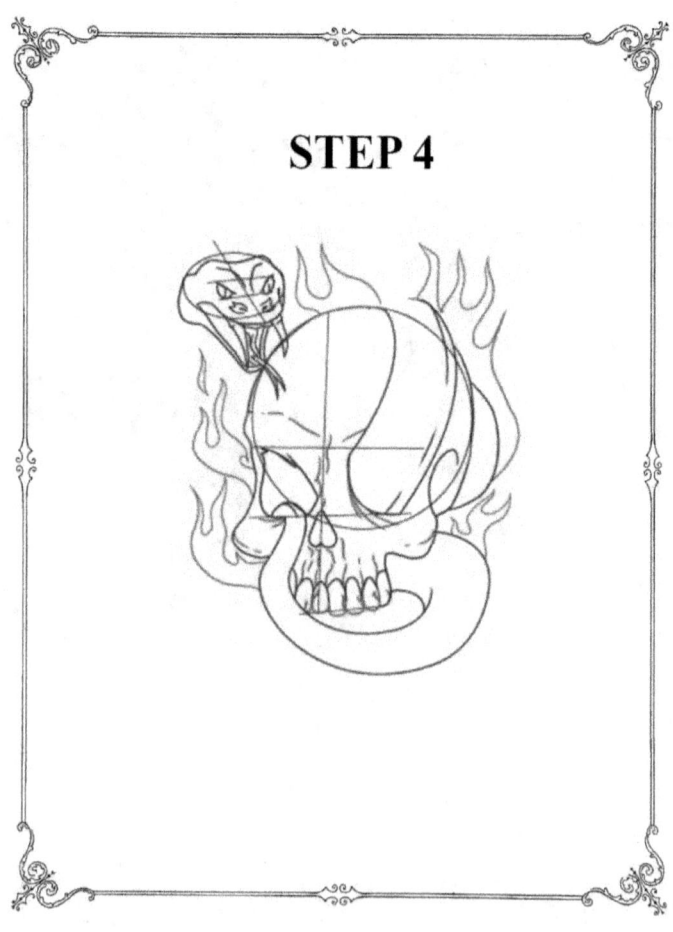

STEP 5

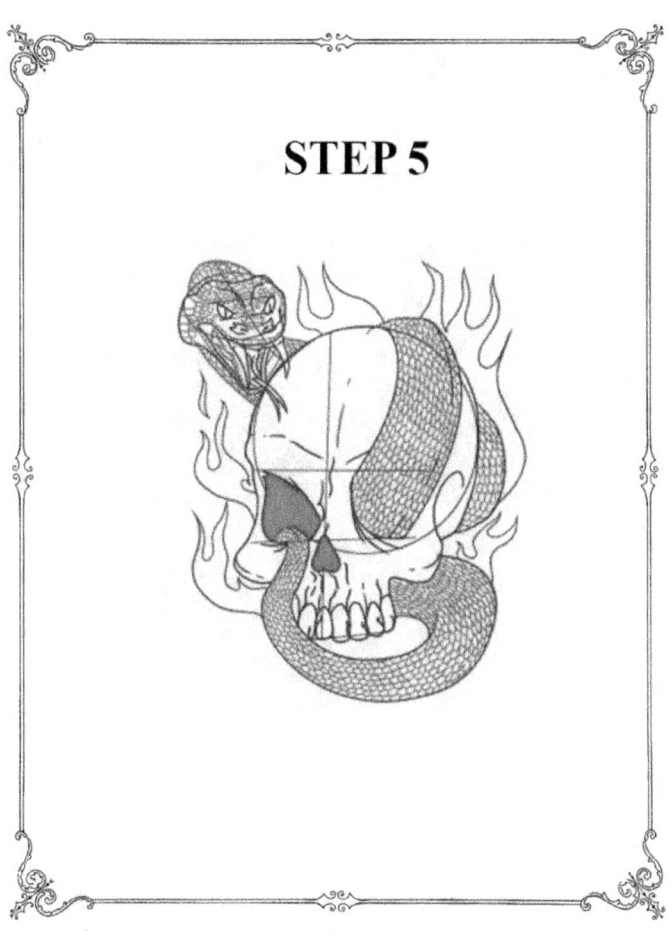

STEP 6

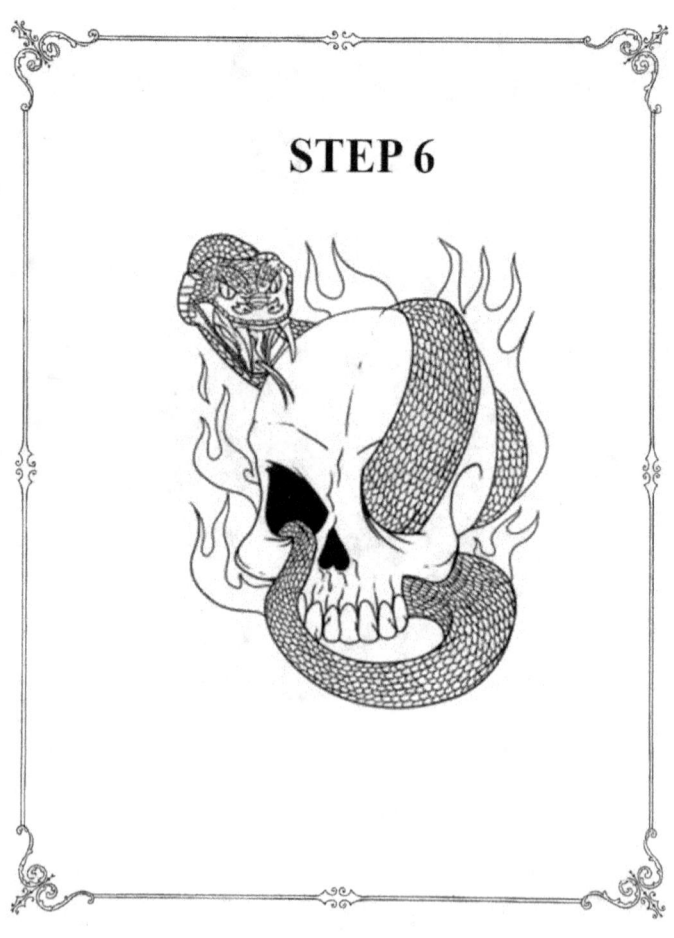

DRAGON SKULL

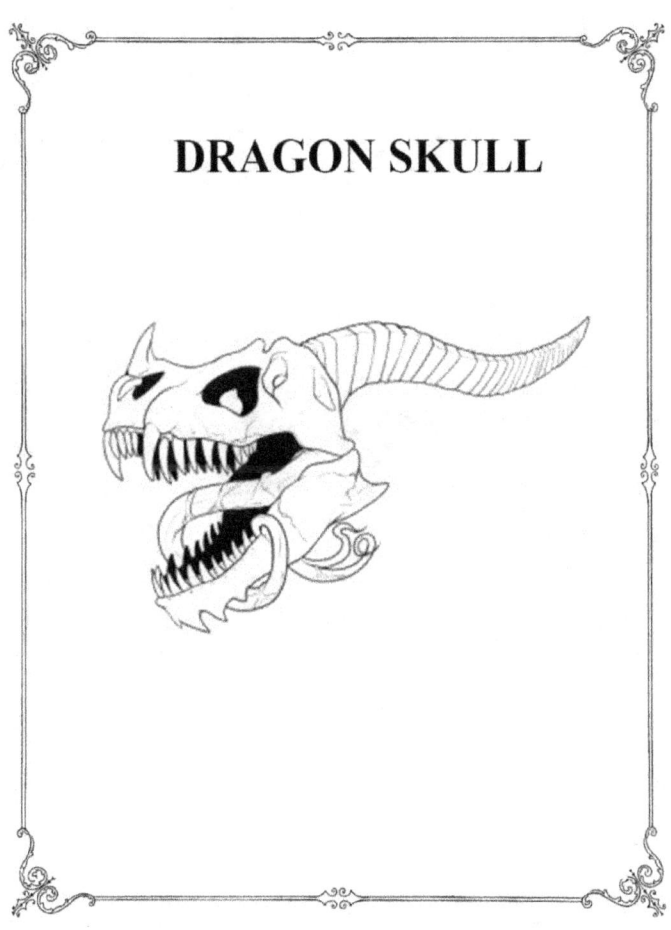

20

STEP 1

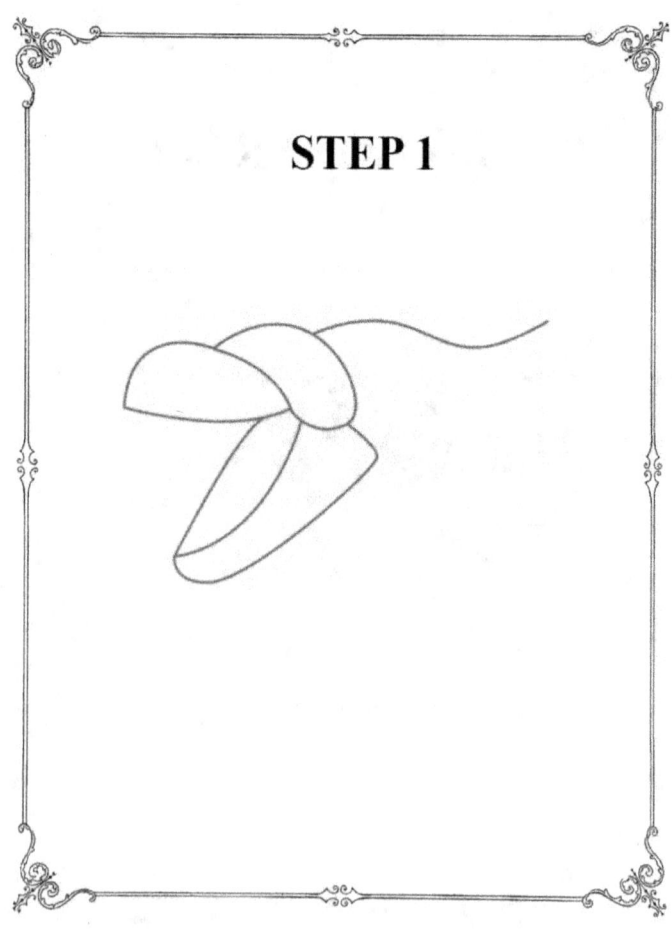

STEP 2

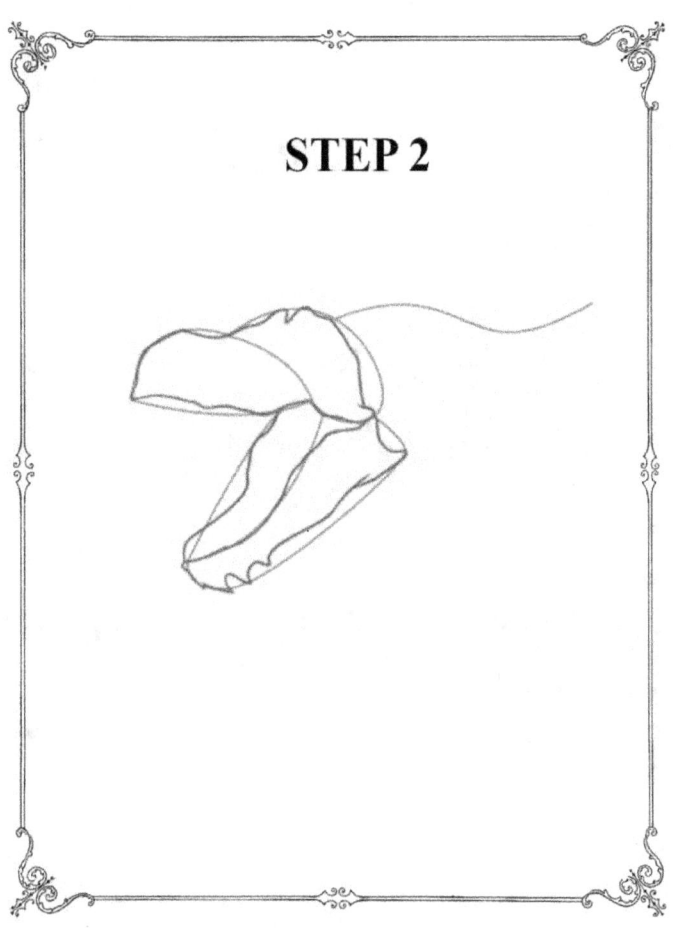

STEP 3

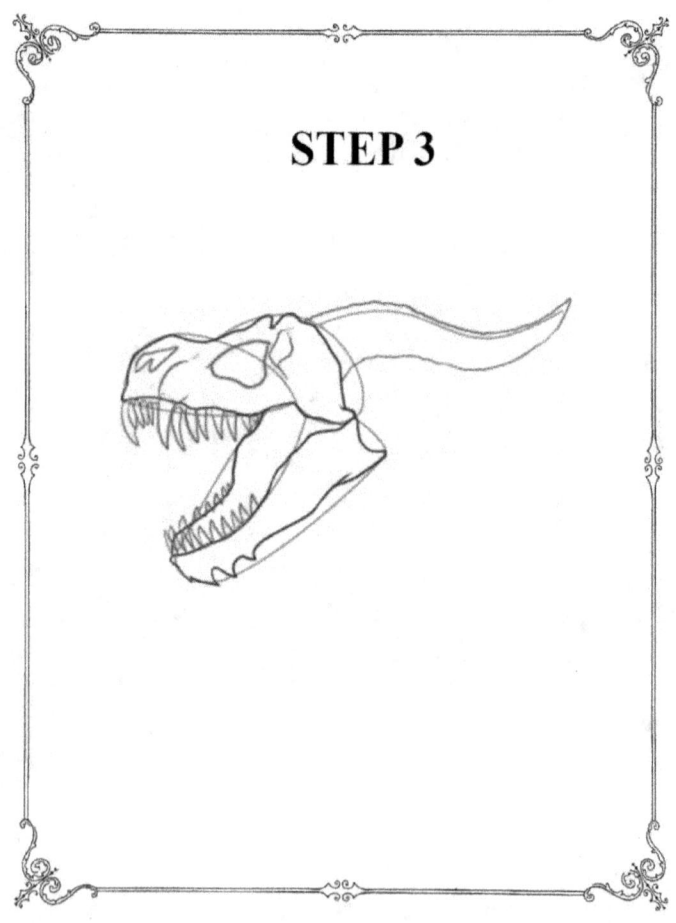

STEP 4

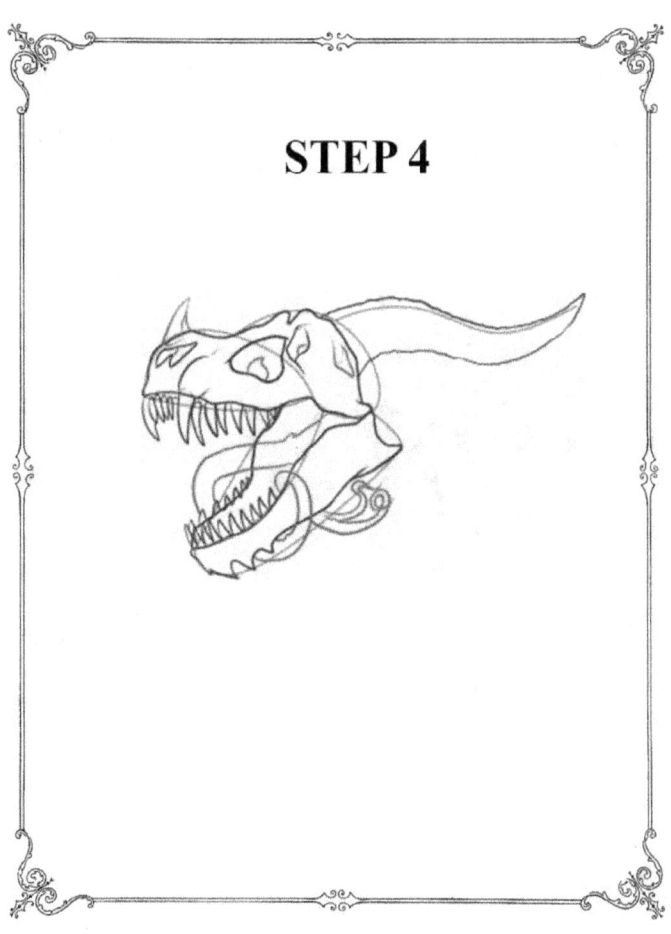

STEP 5

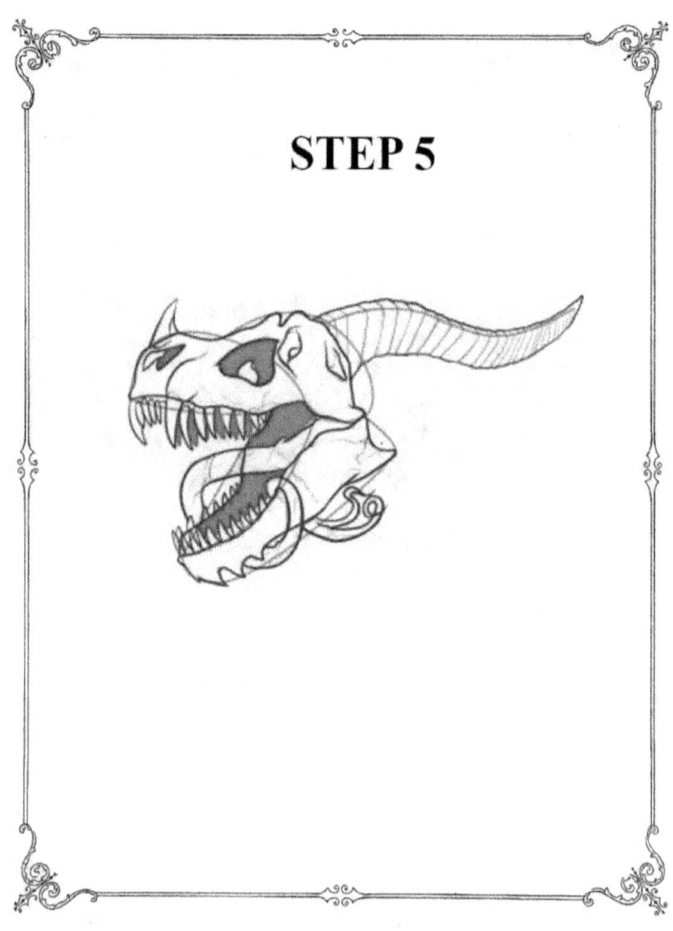

STEP 6

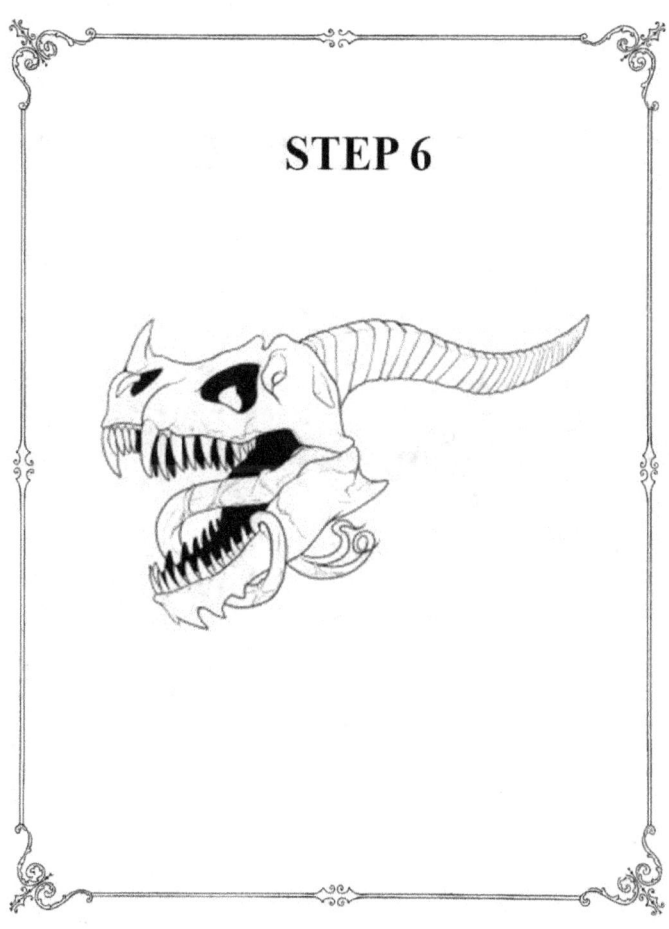

GIRLY SKULL

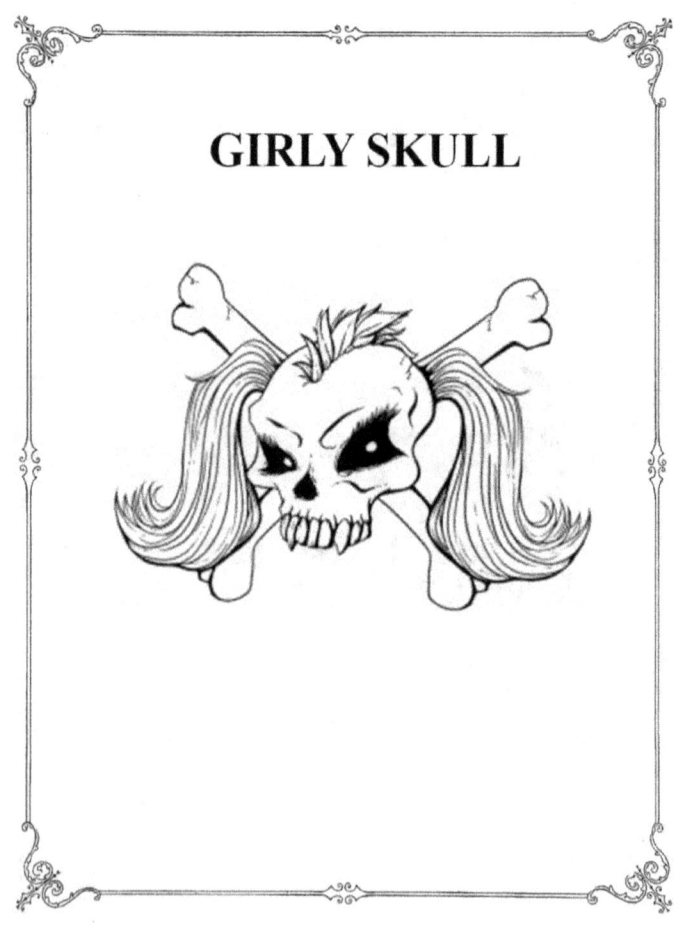

STEP 1

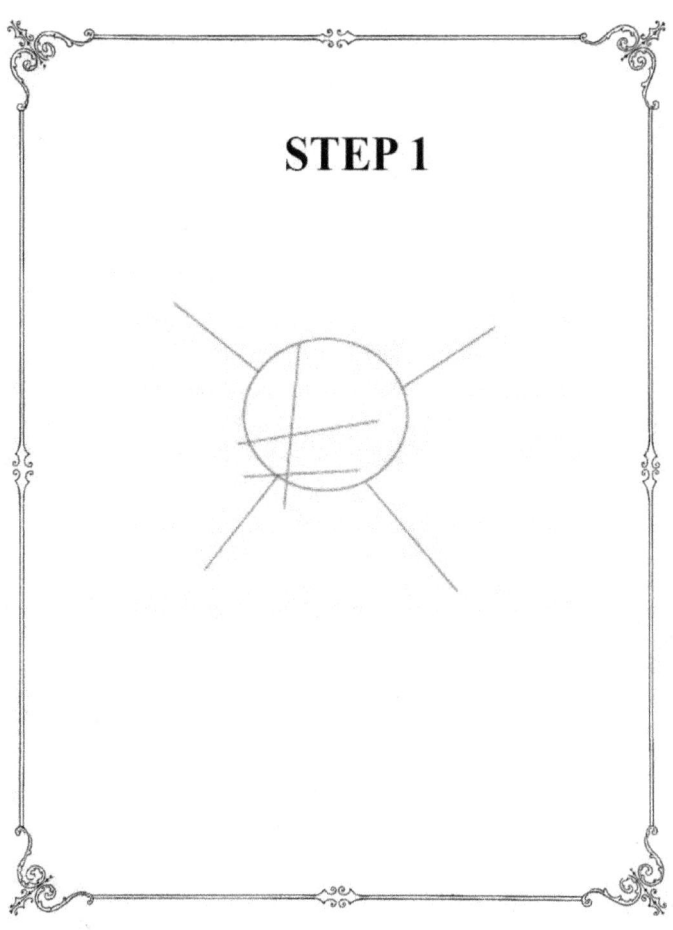

STEP 2

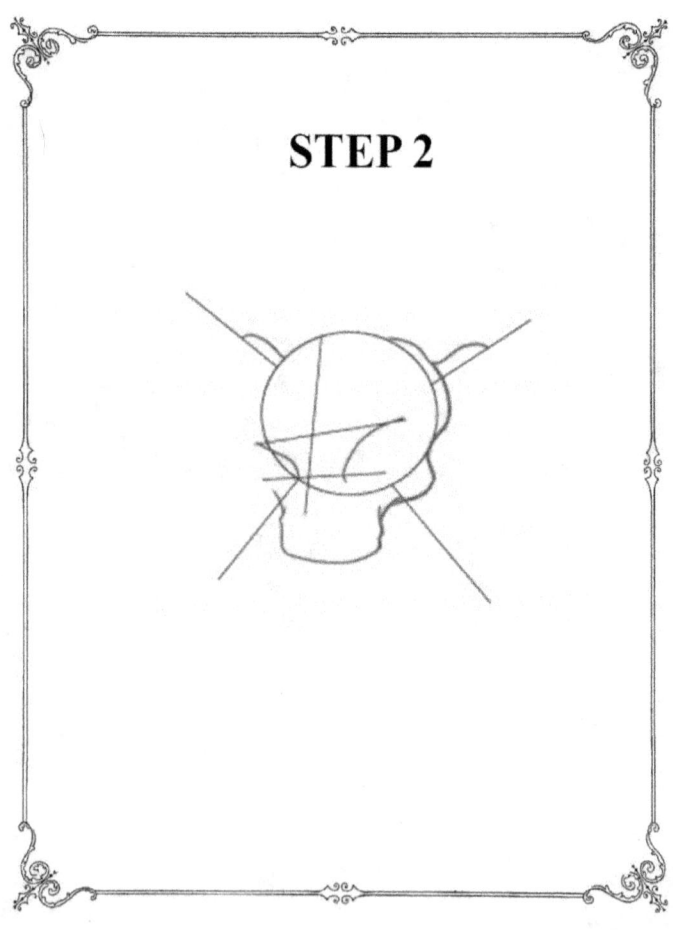

STEP 3

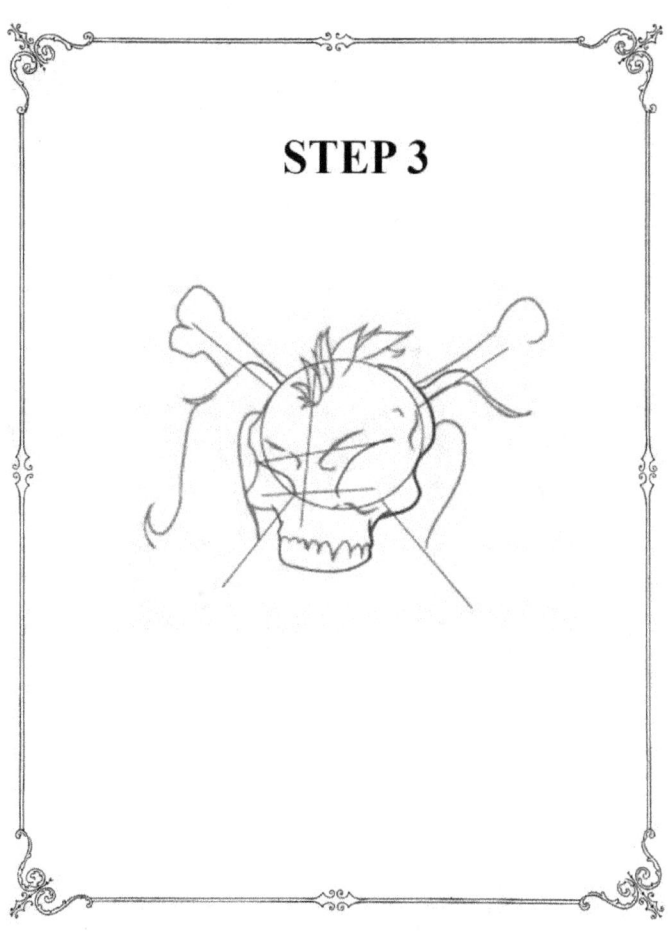

STEP 4

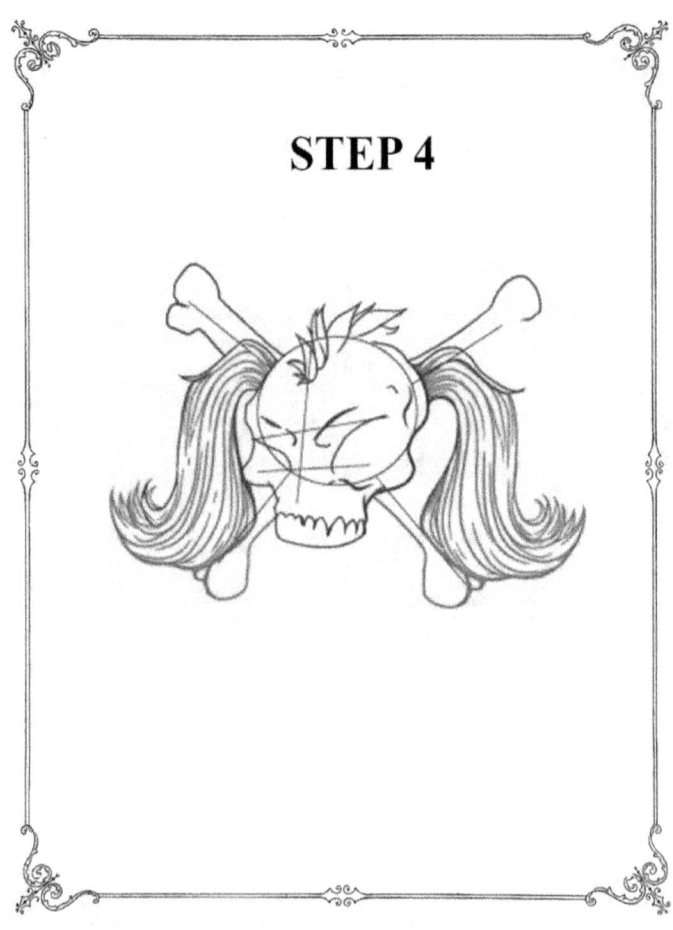

STEP 5

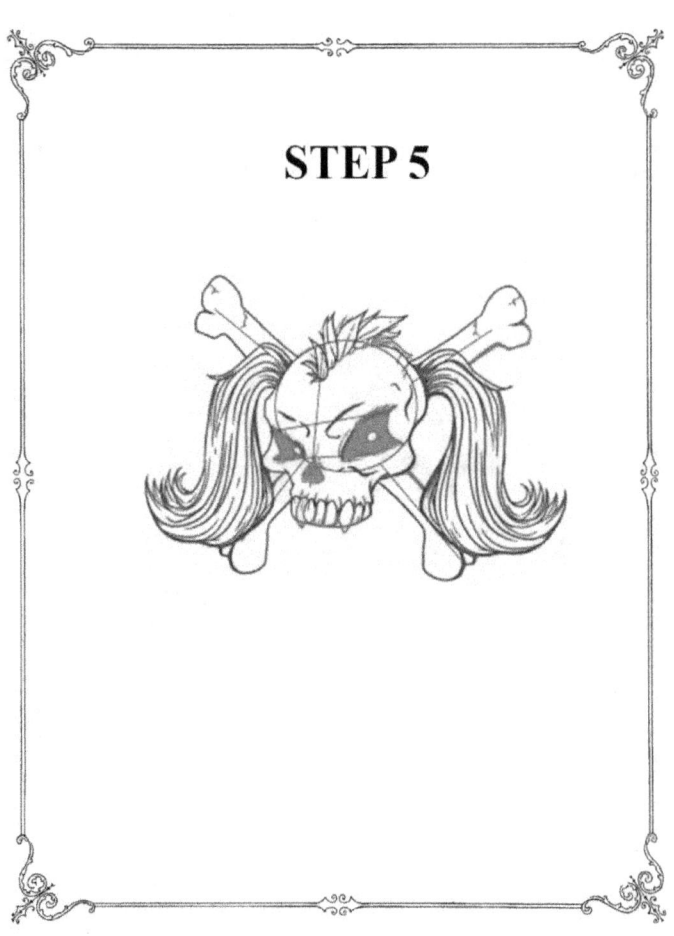

STEP 6

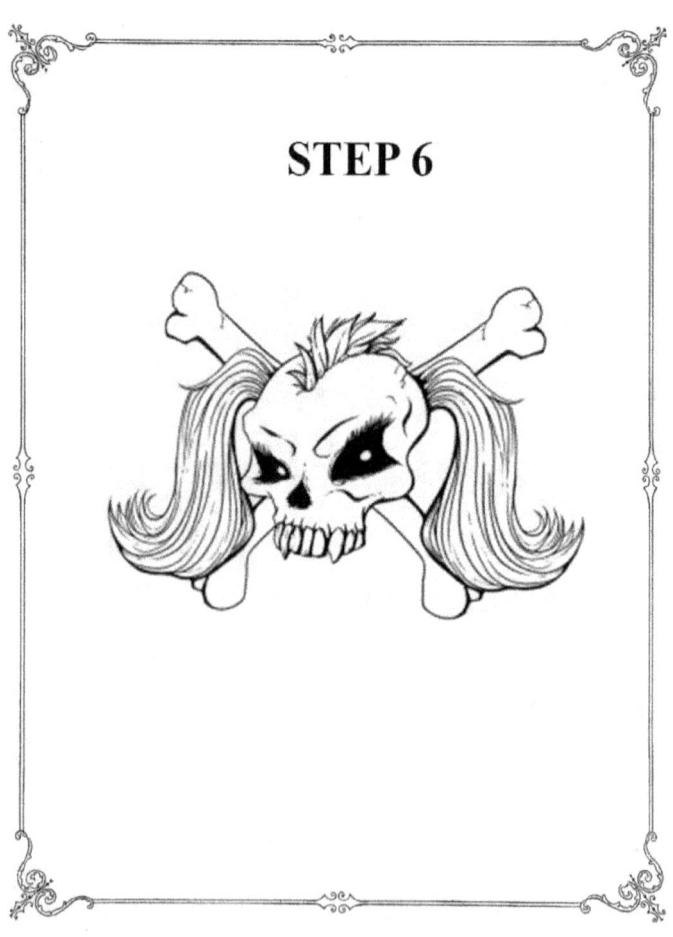

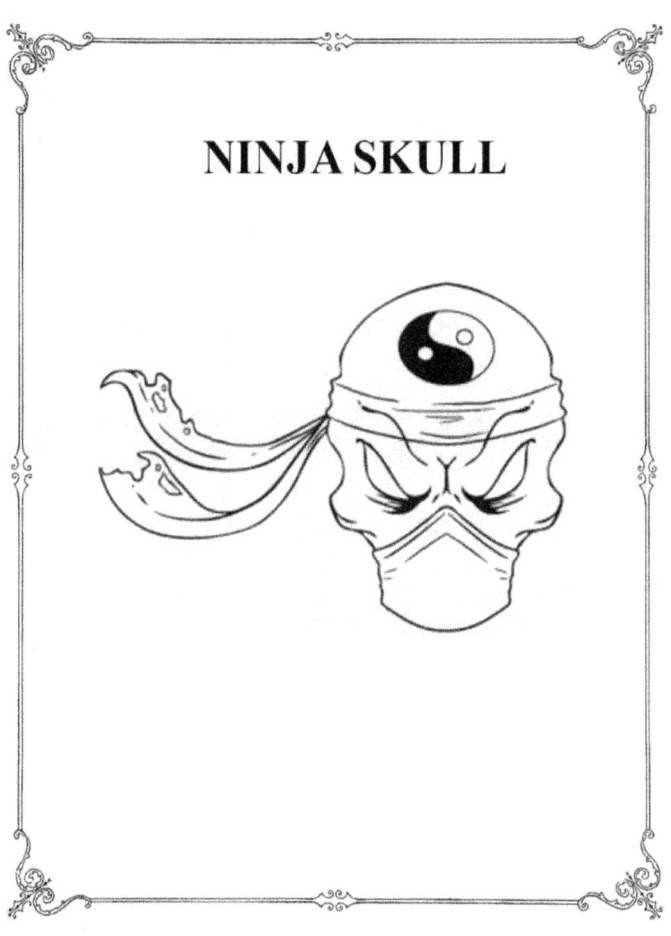

NINJA SKULL

STEP 1

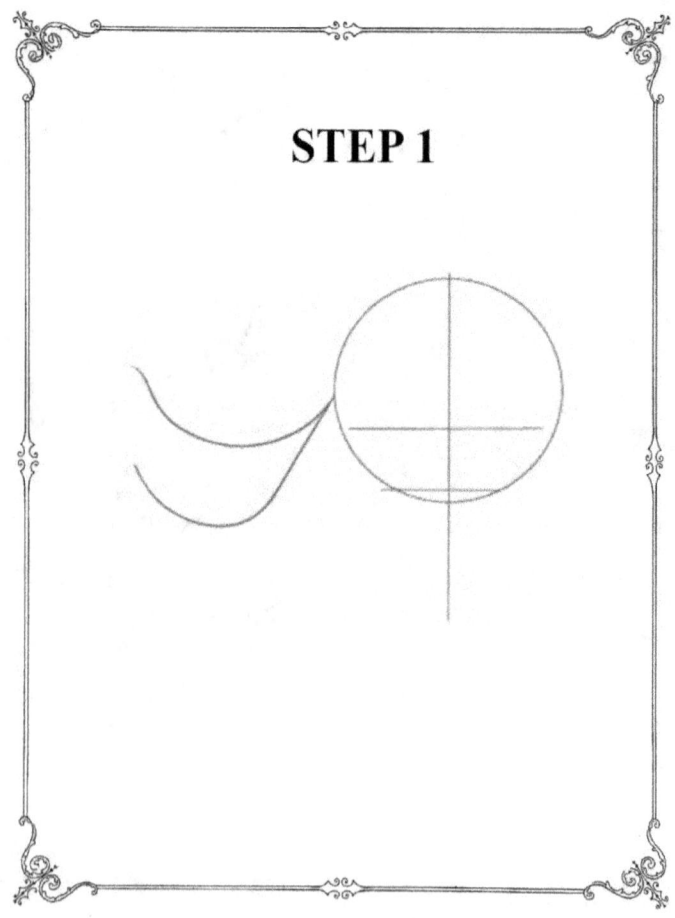

STEP 2

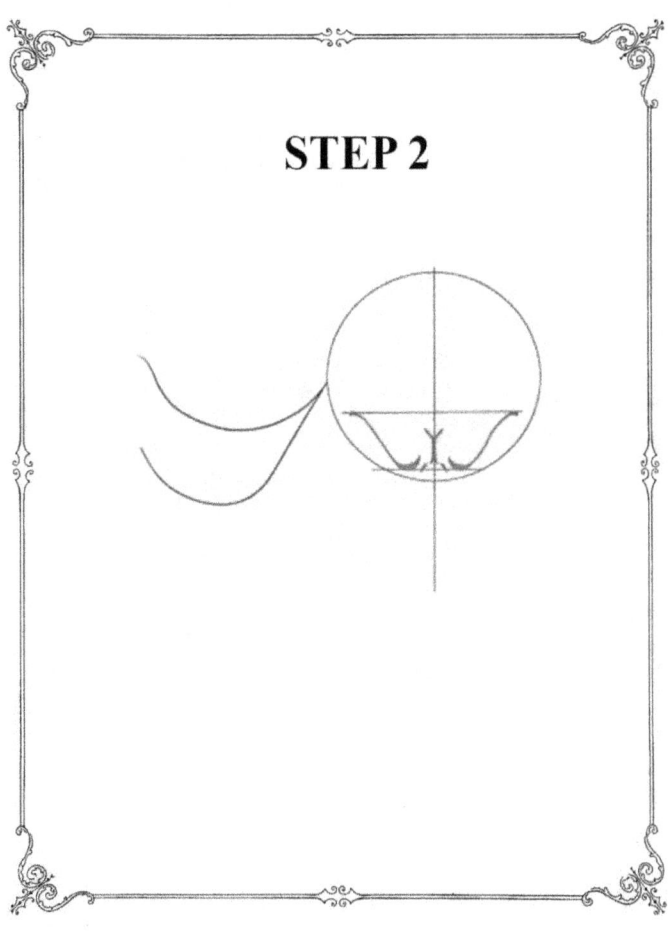

STEP 3

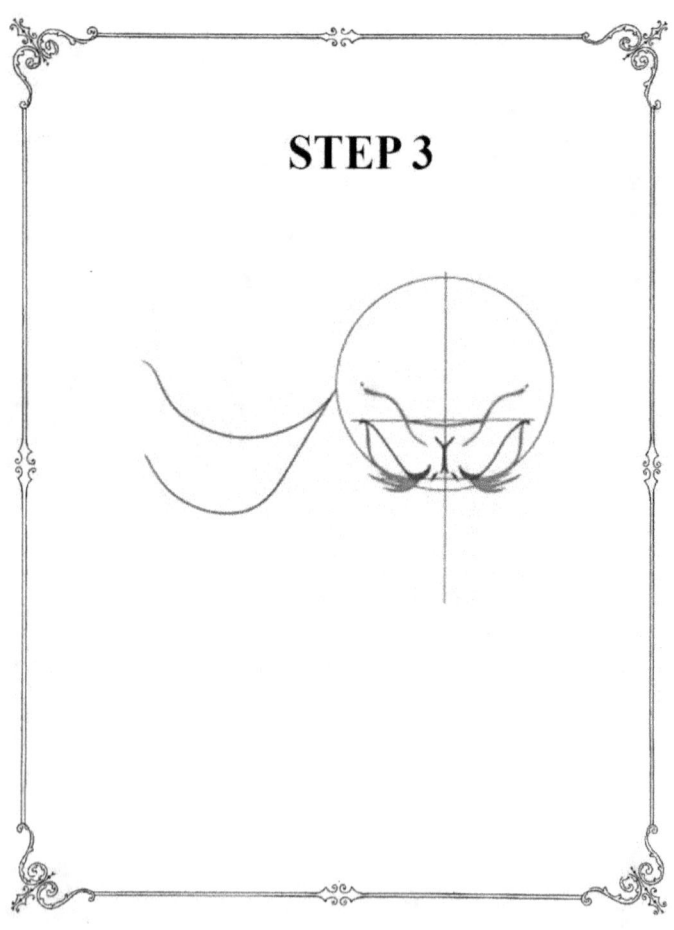

STEP 4

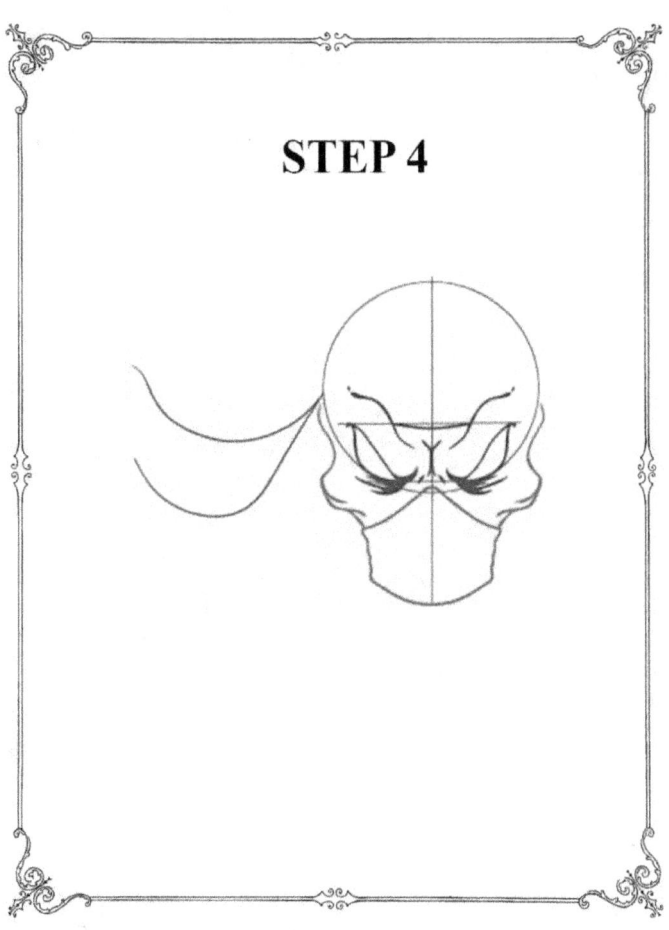

STEP 5

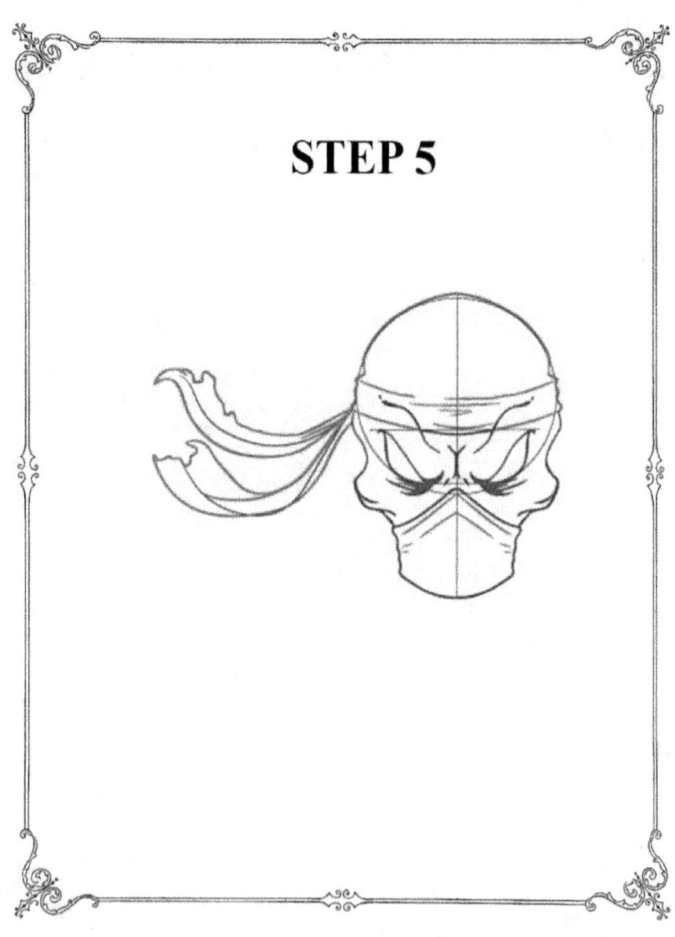

STEP 6

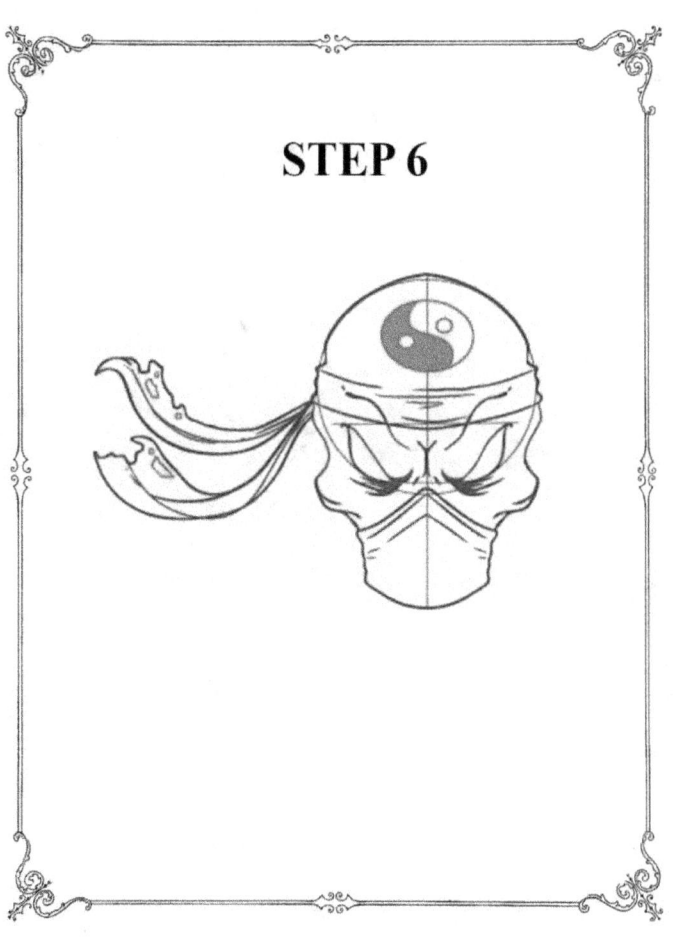

STEP 7

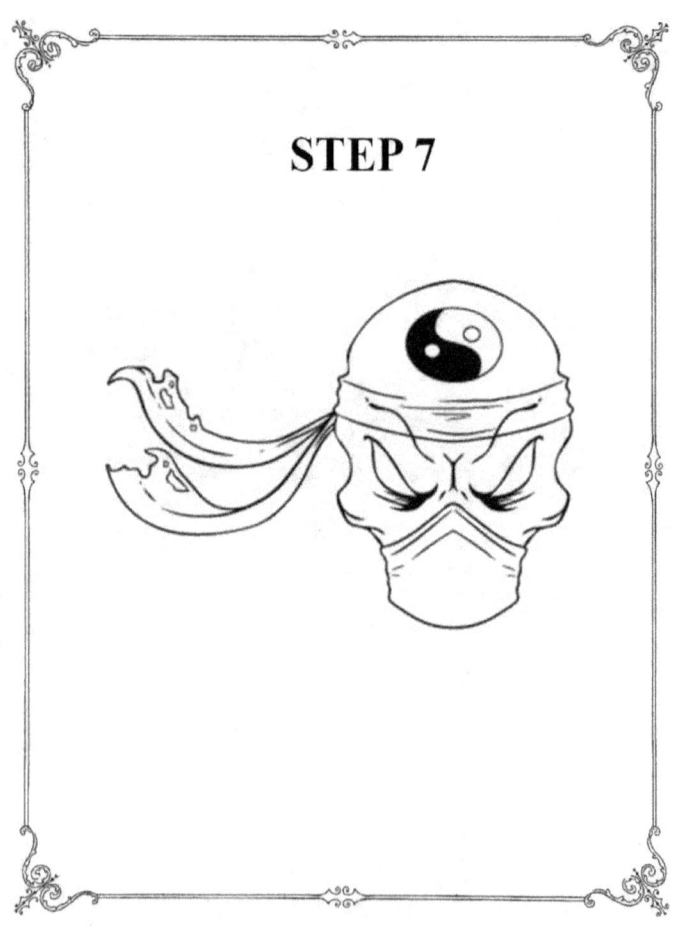

PILOT SKULL

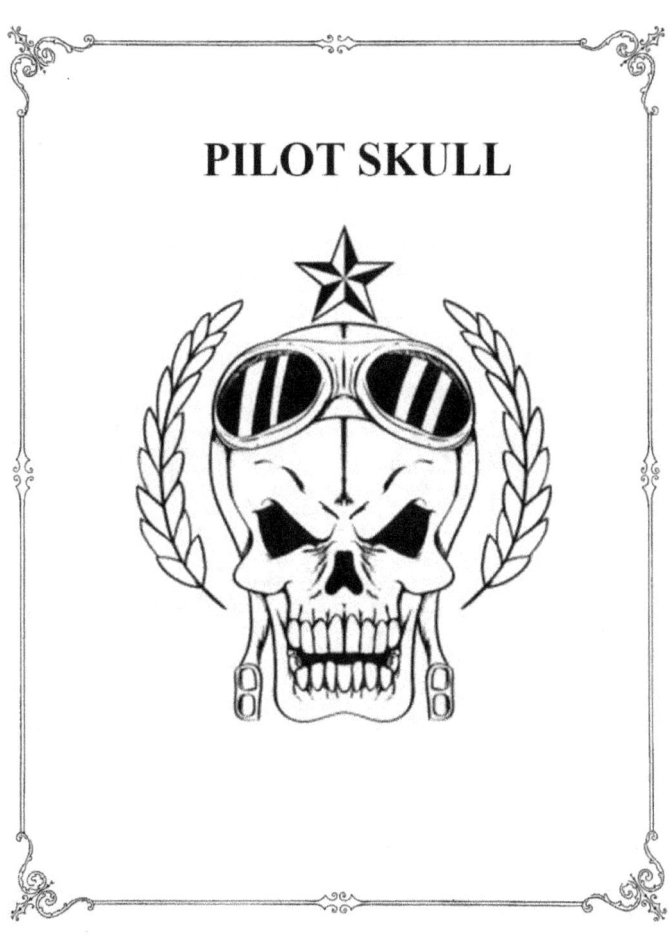

STEP 1

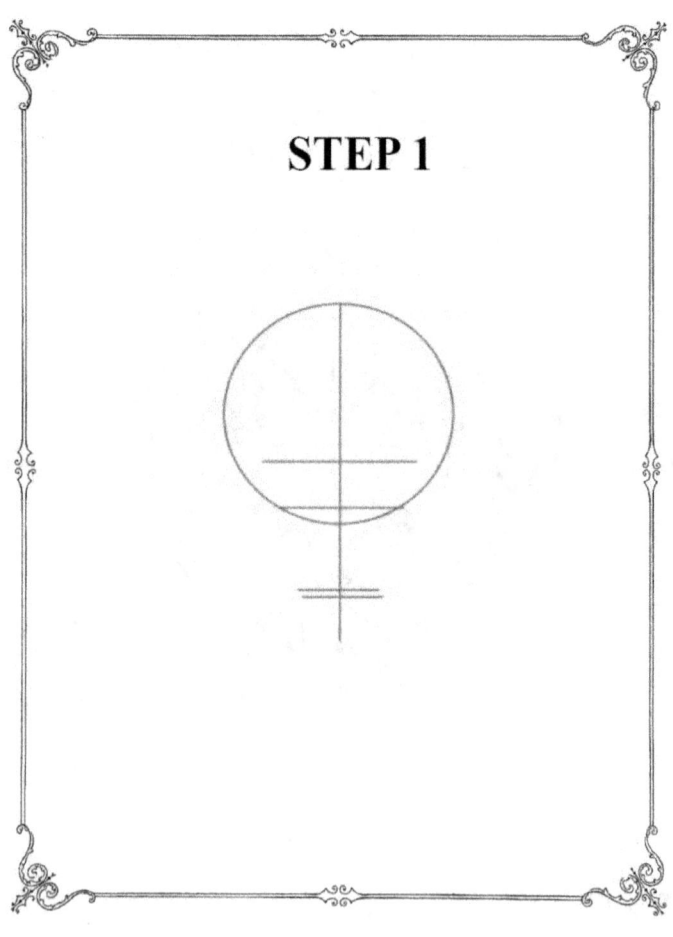

STEP 2

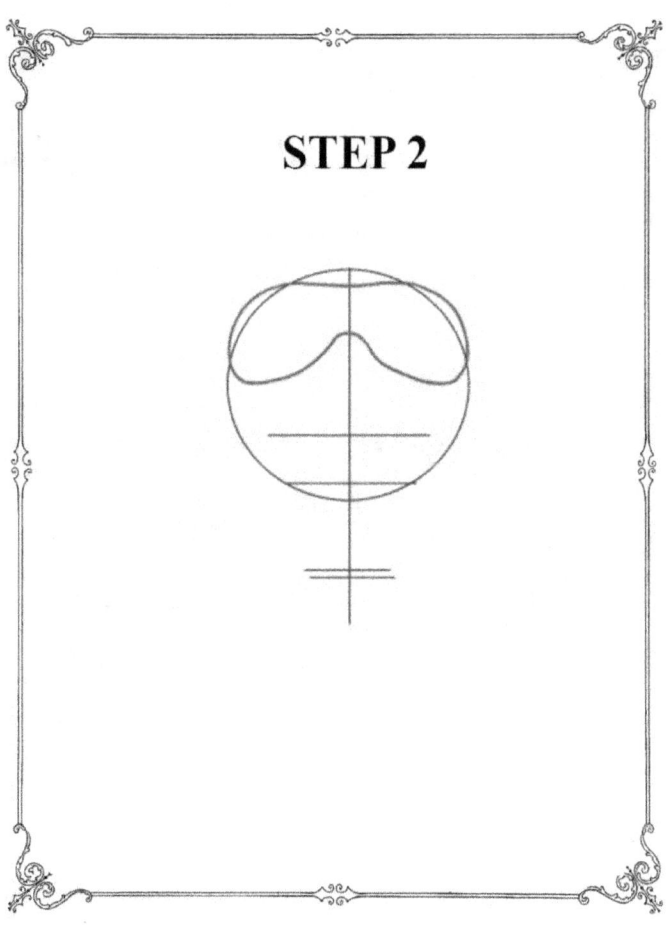

STEP 3

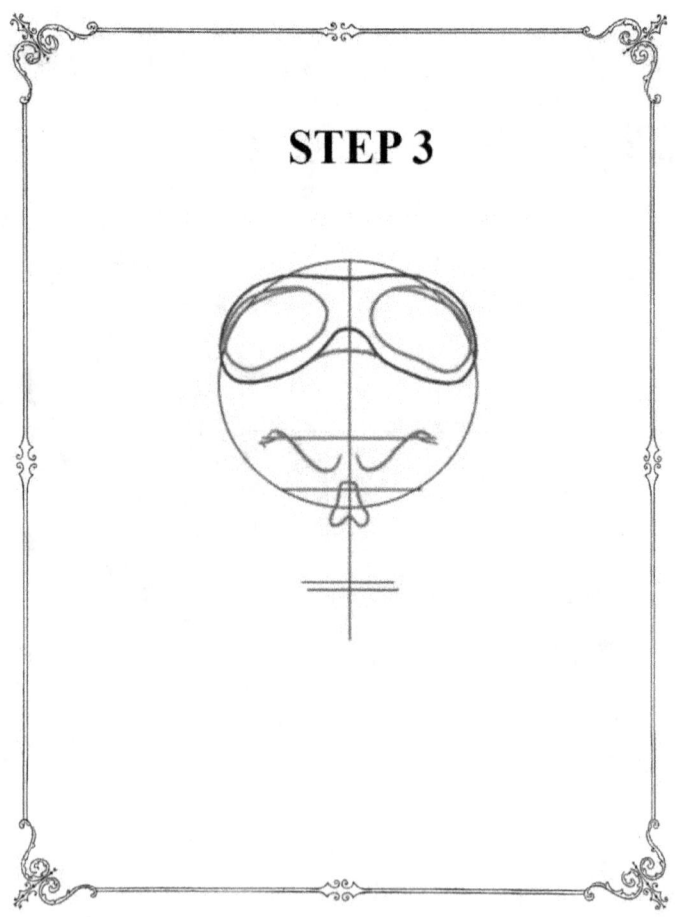

STEP 4

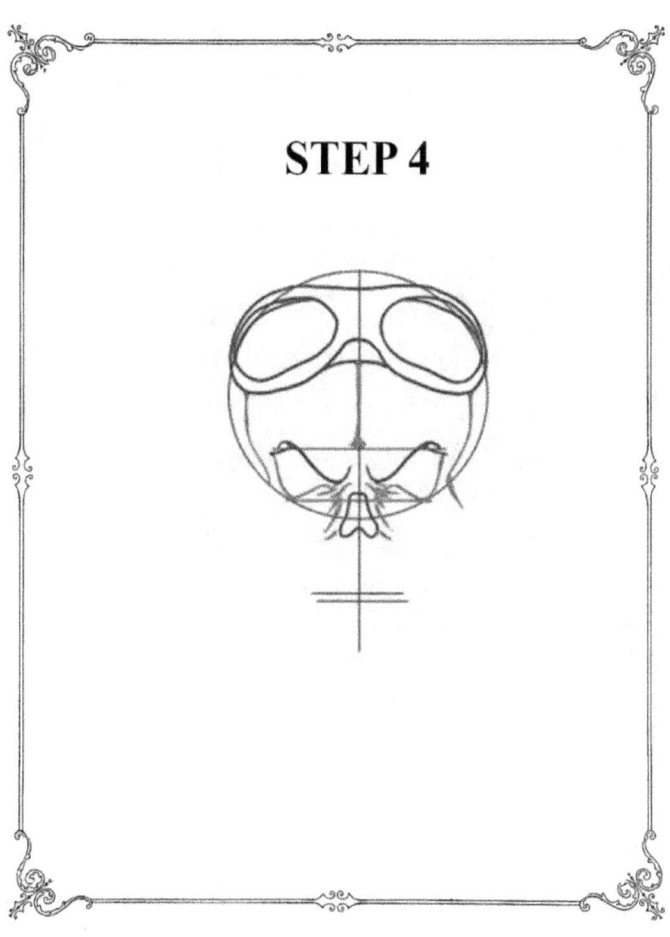

STEP 5

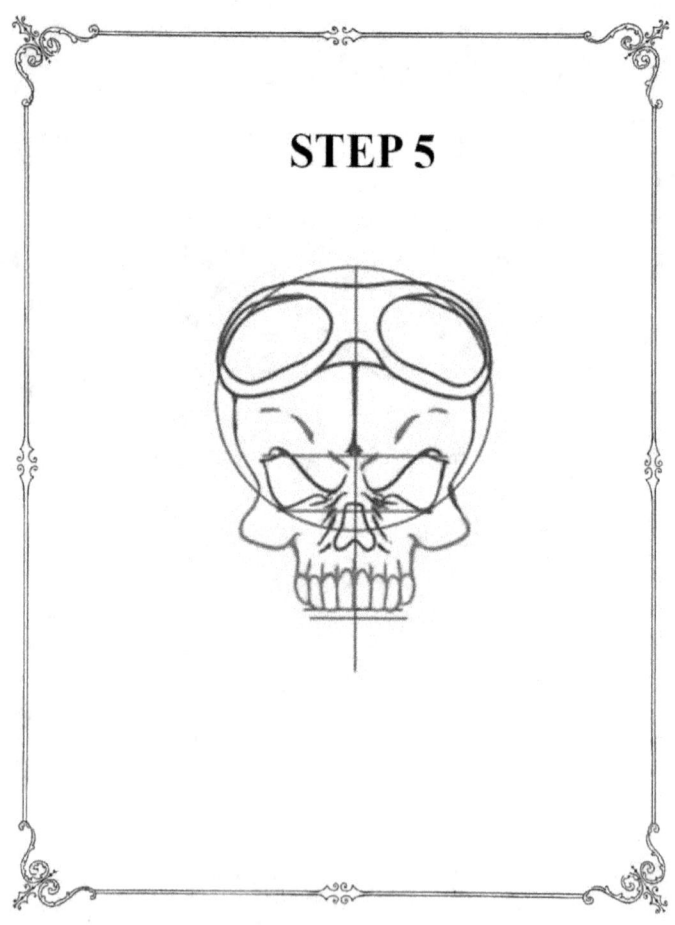

STEP 6

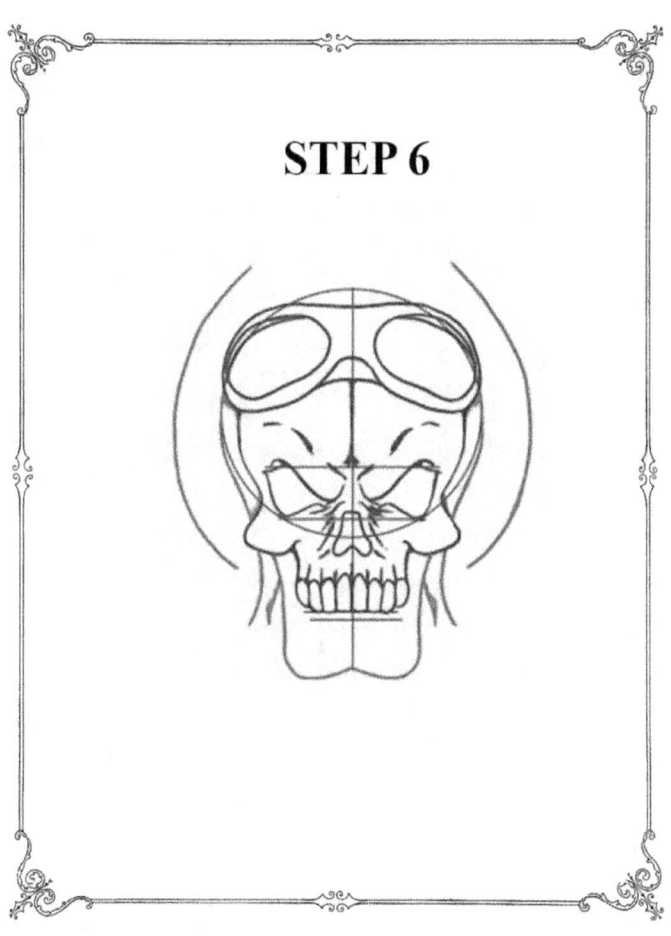

STEP 7

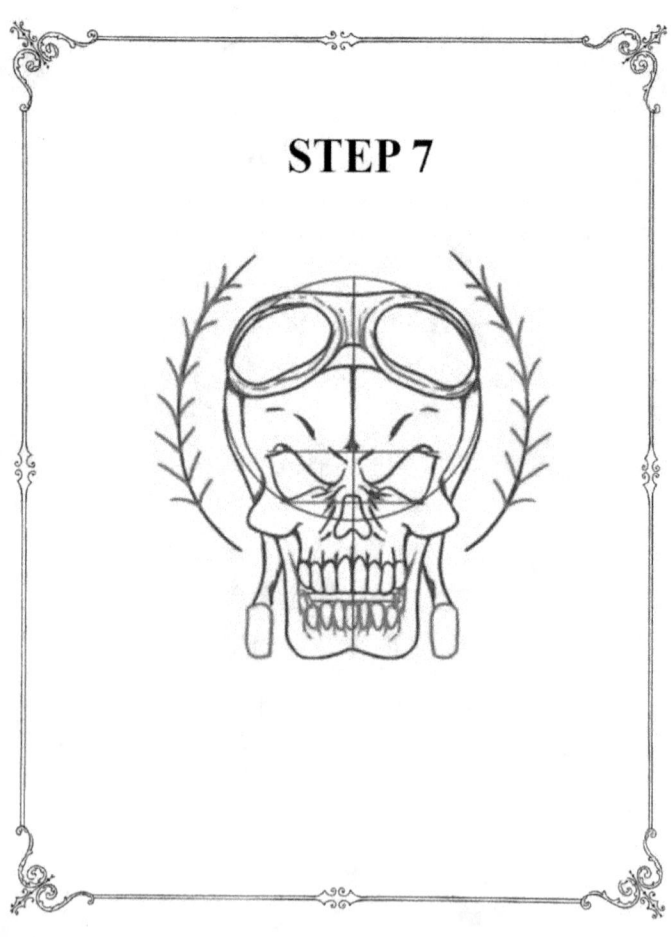

STEP 8

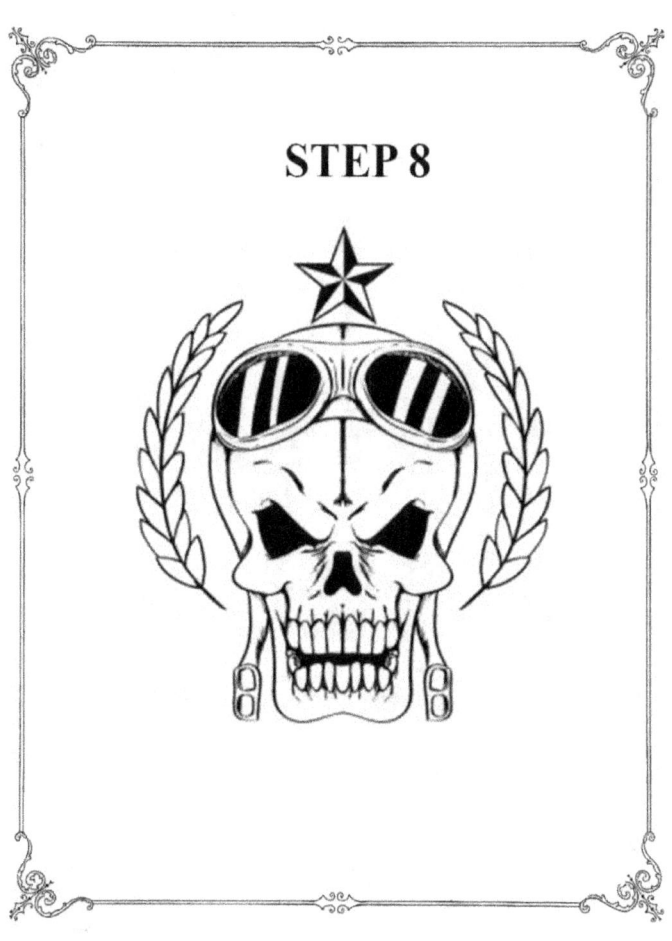

www.ingramcontent.com/pod-product-compliance
Lightning Source LLC
Chambersburg PA
CBHW072029190526
45166CB00015B/1493